Don't Ask Me To Clean Up The Basement

Don't Ask Me To Clean Up The Basement

Hume Cronyn

mosaic press

Library and Archives Canada Cataloguing in Publication

Cronyn, Hume, 1957-
   Don't ask me to clean up the basement / Hume Cronyn.

Poems.
ISBN 978-0-88962-899-1

   I. Title.

PS8555.R6112D65 2009   C811'.54   C2008-908116-1

No part of this book may be reproduced or transmitted in any form, by any means, electronic or mechanical, including photocopying and recording, information storage and retrieval systems, without permission in writing from the publisher, except by a reviewer who may quote brief passages in a review.

Published by Mosaic Press, offices and warehouse at 1252 Speers Rd., units 1 & 2, Oakville, On L6L 5N9, Canada and Mosaic Press, PMB 145, 4500 Witmer Industrial Estates, Niagara Falls, NY, 14305-1386, U.S.A.

info@mosaic-press.com
Copyright © Hume Cronyn, 2009

ISBN 978-0-88962-899-1

Mosaic Press in Canada:
1252 Speers Road, Units 1 & 2,
Oakville, Ontario
L6L 5N9
Phone/Fax: 905-825-2130
info@mosaic-press.com

Mosaic Press in U.S.A.:
4500 Witmer Industrial Estates
PMB 145, Niagara Falls, NY
14305-1386
Phone/Fax: 1-800-387-8992
info@mosaic-press.com

www.mosaic-press.com

ACKNOWLEDGEMENTS

Some of the poems in this collection have appeared in the following publications: *The Cuckoo's Nest, Dog, Grain, Slow Dancer* and the anthology *Kiss Me You Mad Fool*

OTHER BOOKS BY HUME CRONYN

Kiss Me You Mad Fool (edited by *Hume Cronyn*), (Parkdale Activity and Recreation Centre, 1991)

Birdhouse Contributions (Slow Dancer Press, 1993)

Bake My Brain (Mosaic Press, 1993)

Voices of Conscience: Poetry of Oppression (edited by *Hume Cronyn, Richard McKane, Stephen Watts*), (Iron Press, 1995)

Rotten Poetry Fish, (Mosaic Press, 2000)

CONTENTS

I

Morning Blues	4
A Day with My Refrigerator	5
This Moment, So Perfect But	6
Yellow Raincoat	8
Household of Flies	10
Aspirations	12

II

I Won't Even Tell My Mother My Age, God I Must Be Sick	14
Naphthalene Blues	15
Two Days	16
The Day My Sister Told Me She Was a Dog	17
Elephant Poem	19
The Bones of My Mother	21

III

Starbucks' Holiness	24
Break My Life	26
When She Senses I Need Space We Sit at Different Tables	27
Santa Is Black & a Woman & Shoppers of the Dufferin Mall Have Seen the Light	28
Blind Man	30
The Mother of Jeff Buckley Laments	32

IV

Stigma	34
"Will You Take Me Home with You?"	36
Safety in the Streets	38
Ballad of a Bag Man	39

Pop a Pill   42
Miracle of a Warm Cob   44
How He Got There   46
Parc Camping Trip(II)   48

V

An Ordinary Evening   51
Song of Solidarity   52
Pears   53
Walking on Water   54
Praise Poem   55
Lake Muskoka   56

VI

Walk Down the Milky Way   59

I

Morning Blues

I woke up this morning.
My dreams hung on the clothesline
like frozen underwear in a snow storm.

My stomach felt like a boiling pot of stewed tomatoes.
I rushed for the toilet
but all I could find was the sink.

The shower dribbled like a wet handkerchief.

I hastily put on my clothes.
They clung to my body like slimy fish.

I broke an egg into the frying pan.
It sizzled & spattered
in a jumble of soap suds.

I talked to my wife.
She was silent like a chair with a broken leg.

My son jumped out of bed.
He asked me, How do spiders breathe
& do leaves talk to each other at night?
I popped several vitamin pills

& rushed out the front door.
The door followed me to work.
When I wanted it to be closed, it was open;
when I wanted it to be open, it was closed.

Tomorrow, I'm not getting up.

Hume Cronyn

A Day with My Refrigerator

I've spent the day rearranging the refrigerator.

I put love on the first shelf,
but it puddled the plate glass like overdue goat's milk.

I put laughter in the freezer,
but it turned black & opened like a duck's egg.

Truth, I wanted to keep with the lemons,
but it stank of fish & kept me awake.

I delicately placed a balanced personality in the crisper,
but like a coconut its watery milk leaked through its eyes.

I put my favourite chair on the second shelf,
but its legs grew weak & its springs gored a few friends who came to visit.

Between the ketchup & marmalade, I squeezed in a few remembered dreams,
but they grew mouldy & cantankerous & thumped at the door.

Where would I put compassion?
The third shelf brought out its axe & chased it away.

My children, I wanted to put them with the juices.
They had other ideas & climbed the tree outside.

Sleep, it was to have the most privileged place.
It bellowed like a cabbage riddled with worms.

Enthusiasm, too many people keep it with the salami,
I placed it next to the processed cheese & it rotted to the bone.

What to do with honesty, discipline, solitude, anger?
Please, don't ask me clean up the basement.

This Moment, So Perfect   But

It's snowing
I'm sitting outside on a bench
Taking off my skates
My twin sons are still on the rink
One is practicing his slapshot
The other practicing his dekes
It's snowing
We have shoveled off the rink twice in the past hour
A floodlight on a 30 foot post illuminates this neighbourhood rink, no
    boards, just four foot snowbanks
My one son in red sweatshirt & toque
The other in blue sweatshirt & toque
They have always dressed differently
The snow falls, tiny flakes of snow, it falls but never seems to reach the
    ground, we're in a timeless world
The light shines
The willow, with its yellow branches, radiant in the light
My one son in red
The other in blue
This moment, so perfect   But

I am not saving the whales
I am not saving the wolves of Ontario
I am not saving the ozone layer
I am not saving the old forests of Temagami, the Oak Ridges Moraine
I am not saving a single child from the violence of poverty

The snow is falling, in the light it looks like diamonds, gust of wind
    & it blows sideways
My one son hits the top right-hand shelf of the net & whoops with
    triumph
The other cuts one way, then the other, stick blade cuddling the puck
I'm holding my skates in my hand
They're slowly filling with snow
My bare hands glowing with warmth
My one son in red
The other in blue
Two shovels rest side by side, stuck in the snow bank
One shovel is red
The other is blue
This moment, so perfect   But

Hume Cronyn

What am I doing to save the homeless person from a frozen death
What am I doing to save the planet from nuclear extinction
What am I doing to save Somalia/Sudan/Ethiopia from another
    famine
What am I doing to protest the Summit of the Americas

It's snowing
I'm sitting on a bench
My skates are filling with snow
My hands are glowing with warmth
A few wrinkled leaves still cling to the oak tree
It's Friday night, almost eleven o'clock, in a few minutes the floodlight
    will snap off
All week I've worked, much sitting, stale air, too many words
I sit here in silence
The snow whirring & flourishing in this open space
Behind me the road, my car parked on the side, but it could be ten
    miles away
The road that leads home, the road that goes to work, the road that
    leads to love & death & hunger & fear & anxieties, that road stilled
Snow, stillness of snow, nourisher of quiet contemplation
Empty boxes of fruit juice lie scattered at my feet Who could litter this
    sacred space Why is it not considered sacred space

The snow keeps falling
In the light it loses its whiteness, achieves transparency
How long have I been sitting here
My sons finally shout, Dad, let's go
Snow, the beautiful lamb of snow, beyond time, in time, we're covered in
    snow
Call us snowmen of chance
Snowmen of love
Snowmen of luck
Snowmen of small pleasures

The whales must be saved
The wolves must be saved
The ozone layer must be saved
The trees must be saved
The Oak Ridges Moraine must be saved
The planet must be saved from nuclear extinction
Somalia/Sudan/Ethiopia must be saved   But

Perfect moments like this must also be saved

                      Don't Ask Me

Yellow Raincoat

One day, rushing out the door,
it was raining
& I had no raincoat,
raining,
& raining on a bald head
is like a hammer
tapping
on a fragile egg,
so I grabbed my daughter's
yellow raincoat,
one of those Canadian Tire specials,
it had a hood
& a peeked visor
that kept the rain
from piling up
on my bushy eyebrows.

Was it small?
She's only twelve,
it almost fit me perfectly,
except the arms
which slid up
to my elbows.
Shapeless yellow raincoat,
two pockets
large enough
to stuff in uncovered hands,
two pockets,
one,
with bus transfer & string,
probably will be there
till the end of coat.

Yellow raincoat,
I wore it once,
then twice,
I even wore it when it wasn't raining,
my daughter stopped asking
for it back,
how many early mornings

Hume Cronyn

I trudged to work,
place of smoke & hunger,
I hung it from a coat peg,
it took on the smell of smoke
& windowless room,
it grew breathless,
squashed between coats
& bags.

But, once outside,
how it sprung free!
Some days it blossomed
like a daffodil,
wonder of fiery petals,
another day
it was a yellow bell
& I tinkled
all the way down the street,
& other days,
in the deep, deep rain,
I was a yellow submarine
but, because I had no need to rhyme,
I was not sailing to a sea of green,
I was just a yellow submarine
sailing down the streets of Parkdale,
& if I was singing,
it's for a love of being submerged,
& who knows?
next day I may be a piece of the sun,
or the jubilant blazing
of a full moon.

Yellow raincoat!
Shine on! Shine on!
You strip me of my black clothes,
my smoky thoughts,
my hundred-fold hungers.
When I wear you,
I am windows & sky,
the glorious tinkling of bells,
flower announcing the end of winter,
& the pure joy
of being a yellow submarine.

Household of Flies

Because we had missed several weeks of pickup,
the garbage accumulated.
During the day we'd put the bags outside;
during the night we'd bring them back in
to keep them from being ripped apart by raccoons.

The garbage bags began to feel like pets that we'd put out for the day
& bring in each night.
God knows, one day we'll bring up the leash
from the basement & take one for a walk.
I can imagine people stopping us:
Ho, what a nice dog you have! What kind is it?
Oh, it's a rare breed, a garbage hound,
unfortunately, it never knows when to stop eating,
it's impossible to locate its feet.

One night we brought the bags in,
they were multiplying like rabbits,
one of the bags unknotted itself:
a gush of maggots spilled out.

Now, we have a household of flies.
Even in my most Zen-like moods, I cannot consider flies as pets.
Today, I can't stand it any longer.
Hundreds of flies buzzing against the windows,
congregating on the blades of the kitchen fan,
the bare light bulb in the basement,
&, oddly enough, a mass of them clinging to the smoke detector that hangs
    open from the ceiling.
Flies in my lemonade, flies in the washing machine as I throw in my clothes,
flies ricocheting around the lampshade as I turn off the light,
flies that dive-bomb me as I sleep,
flies that crawl into my apple crumble,
flies that finger the gobs of toothpaste streaking the sink.

I couldn't take it any longer.
I grabbed the Business Section of *The Globe & Mail*,
rolled it up & began to whack,
I began in the basement, they were pressed up against the casement window,
whack, whack, smashed bodies tumbled into the wash basin below.

Hume Cronyn

I was furious when I saw some hiding in the stack of freshly-folded clothes,
I jabbed at them & when they flew upwards
I started swatting them with a crazed ferocity,
half-laughing at myself for such futility.

I went upstairs. My son joined me with a rolled-up newspaper.
God knows where the fly swatter is? (It was last seen nestled in my daughter's
     sock drawer.)
We snuck up on the flies that were a cloud on the living room window, we
     whacked & whacked, blood & wings spotted the window,
a mass of dead flies lay on the carpet.

My other son joined in. The three of us trooped downstairs again.
My sons, not tall enough, had to stand on their tiptoes to swat the flies on
     the ceiling,
they killed at least a dozen
before they knocked down the light fixture.

Mass of dead flies, & still there were flies. When I walked into the furnace
     room, they were plastered against the only window.
When I walked into the garage, as soon as I opened the door,
a cloud of flies flew up, hurling themselves into my face,
one flew into my mouth.

Next morning, not even a glimmer of light on the horizon, I put out the
     garbage.

Aspirations

I don't want to write the Great Canadian novel, the Great Canadian
    story, the Great Canadian bullshit, the Great Canadian palaver,
    the Great Canadian poem,
I don't even want to write the Great Canadian Rice Crispies ad,
I don't want to be the Great Canadian hero, the Great Canadian Bagel,
    the Great Canadian mountain, the Great Canadian Santa Claus,
I don't want to be the Great Canadian anything.

I just want to write a poem so crazy, so off-the-wall that when you hear
    it you think nothing of gluing your ear to the wall & singing songs
    to the birds trapped in that big glob head of yours,
when you hear my poem, you will climb into your freezer & burrow
    into the ice cubes to test the temperature of your burning
    imagination,
when you hear my poem, you will cut out words from the dictionary
    & line your shoes with vatic proclamations,
when you hear my poem, you will grow leaves & rustle in the big
    storm,
when you hear my poem, you will fill your pockets with sand & walk
    around like an untouched beach,
when you hear my poem, you will fry your cell phone in sunflower oil
    & feed it to your sister-in-law who threatens to bite your leg,
when you hear my poem, you will sit on the top shelf of your garage &
    contemplate the solitude of dust,
when you hear my poem, you will knock down all the stop signs & roll
    down the side of a hill like a green torch,
when you hear my poem, you will glitter in the sun like a shattered
    window that rejoices in its open-mouthed hallelujah,
when you hear my poem, you will push up through the pavement &
    dance with dandelion joy,
when you hear my poem, you will throw away your crutches,
    suspenders, shoe laces, toothbrush & live in the fiery firmament
    of your exuberance,
when you hear my poem, you will rip it up & start all over again.

Hume Cronyn

II

I Won't Even Tell My Mother My Age, God I Must Be Sick

My mother, old & crumbly, like dust I could pinch her between my fingers
& she'd float to the ground in feathery specks.
My mother, not so old, nearing 80, two years ago she was young,
her face, nut-brown, one of those faces that seemed ageless,
now her face, crease upon crease,
she reminds me of the 10-year-old walnuts that she leaves around in bowls.
My mother, we're at a restaurant celebrating my daughter's thirteenth
    birthday,
she looks at me, lipstick crawling up the creases of her mouth,
she reminds me of those fruits, where the inside dries out completely,
if you shake it, nothing but the rattling of shriveled seeds.
My mother, she looks at me, her eyes once a depth of brown,
now a screen which so clearly shows her puzzlement,
my mother, she asks me, "How old are you, Hume?"
like her mother, her mind subject to blanks, gaps, black holes of lost memory,
"How old are you?" she asks me, me, who never! never! never! tells my age,
so the one person who knew my age, who gave me age, she no longer knew.
I felt giddy, & you know what? I wouldn't tell her,
then she made a stab in the dark, brightly she named the date of my birth,
it wasn't so easy for her to remember what year it was today,
she made an effort to do the mathematics, she couldn't do it,
simple mathematics, & I wouldn't even help her out.
Sick! man. Sick!
Maybe one day when I'm a blubbering 85,
you'll see me running down the street
hollering at the top of my lungs, I'm 85! I'm 85 glorious, wondrous, difficult
    years!
& I'm not afraid to admit it.

Hume Cronyn

Naphthalene Blues

Mothballs live in my parents' bedroom.
They inundate their drawers,
Cuddle up to socks, underwear, shirts.
Look in their cupboard,
You will find them in the pockets of bathrobes,
    In the hems of dresses,
    In the toe of a stray boot
That's inhabited the cupboard for fifteen years.
Mothballs wedged between stacks of newspapers,
Beneath the cushion of the chaise longue,
Even a lone mothball on the windowsill,
    Mothball, white as a bedridden body.

Don't look under their bed.
Each night the smell of mothballs close my parents' eyes.
They sleep naphthalene sleeps.
They nibble slices of mothball pies.
Mothballs roll down the hills of their dreams,
Mothballs snowball into larger mothballs
    Big as closed fists
    Big as cannonballs
Mothball snowmen
Mothball bowling balls
Mothball tumours large as bowling balls.

Mom dying of leukaemia.
Dad dying of cancer.

Bring back the moths. They don't feed on people.

Two Days

Turquoise blouse Blue blazer draped over her shoulders
She's already been sick into the toilet
Breakfast of shredded wheat & strawberries

She walks unsteadily through the den

He Stain on his blue shirt
Curiously resembles his swollen hand
He waits for her at the door

She slightly cocks the elbow of her right arm
He slides his arm through hers
They take their first steps down the hallway
Almost glide
Like striding down the aisle of their wedding

Toss the confetti
Catch the bouquet
Hoot & holler & blow kisses

Unsteadily they finish their walk down the hall
She's going for blood tests
Two days to live

Hume Cronyn

The Day My Sister Told Me She Was a Dog

All afternoon we shopped at the market:
carrots, apples, ginger, celeriac, beets
& one potato (we laughed at the exactitude of the recipe),
one potato, the size of an egg.
It was all organically grown,
destined for my parents' old juicer.
My sister had purchased a book,
Dr. Breuss' Cancer Cures,
where he solemnly proclaimed
that if a leukemia patient drank
8 oz. of this concoction a day, that
even the sickest patient would be up
& working after a week.

My sister & I had extravagant hopes.
We didn't think that Mom would be cured,
but at least she'd live another six months.
Confound that doctor who told her
she only had two weeks to live.
Damn him! Stuff death up his ass!
Ever since he had told her
(he might as well have kicked her
in the stomach), she'd been in shock.

Before we left the market,
we stopped at a juice bar.
We talked about Mom:
she had not thrown out a paper bag
for twenty-five years; she covered
the couches with sheets to save them
for another twenty-five years,
but the generosity of her love was so profound
that it totally shaped our personalities.
As so often when we got together,
our conversation turned to J.D. Salinger's *Franny & Zooey*,
which Martha had just reread.
My sister lives on her own,
is obsessed with her dog, Heathcliff.
Her hands fluttered as she mentioned
a part in the book where

Zooey claims that each one of us
has an angel in us, but it is so deeply
buried that it rarely makes an appearance.
However, Heathcliff, not burdened by the confines
of society, his angel is apparent in his twinkling eyes,
his crazy grin, & wherever he went
people were quick to recognize his angel
spirit. Why didn't Mom see it?
She hated leaving Heathcliff behind in Toronto.
I told her Mom didn't feel up to seeing him,
but I'm sure she will when she gets a little better.

Leaving the market, we crossed a windswept plaza,
its paving stones, grey as the clouds above, were covered with puddles.
Vendors were hurriedly taking down makeshift stalls.
The thundering sound of a jackhammer filled the afternoon.
As if he had no faith in the sun ever appearing,
a man was drilling channels to drain off the puddles.
We came to the edge of the plaza, stood there
unable to take the first step down the wide-aproned stairs,
stood there transfixed, peering down at a hot dog stand
on the far side of the street, with its trim of lights
flashing in the dull air. Suddenly, a burly,
pony-tailed man trotted out from behind a truck,
pulled towards the hot dog stand by his German shepherd.
The man radiated complete enthrallment with his company.
Martha turned to me & shouted, Heathcliff & I are one!
Well, it was relatively easy to absorb this utterance:
she constantly chatters to him, cooks chicken
& rice for his breakfast, & whenever she cries
Heathcliff licks the tears from her eyes.
But this did not prepare me for her next statement:
I am a dog, she blurted. She said it with such conviction,
I looked at her half-expecting to see a dog.
No kidding, she said, whenever a dog spots me,
he bounds across the street to sniff my leg
& say hello. How unprepared we are
for so many things. Next day, Mom died.

Hume Cronyn

Elephant Poem

Sometimes I lose my elephant for weeks on end.
He wanders amongst the books on my desk.
He wanders amongst the magazines, the scribbled pieces of writing,
    newspaper clippings, half a dozen red pens.
He wanders. Does he miss lumbering through the bamboo forests of
    Rwanda,tramping along the Chobe River of Botswana, swaying
    through the blue-grassed savannas of Zimbabwe?
No! He loves scratching his trunk against the spines of my books, he
    loves hiding behind my chaotic stacks of paper, he rolls my pens
    for fun, I hear him singing out the titles of my books:
Song of the Simple Truth,
Letter to an Imaginary Friend,
Young Poets of New Poland,
Unthinkable Tenderness,
In the Spirit of Crazy Horse,
The Buddhist Third Class Junkmail Oracle
& his favourite, *Set This Book on Fire.*
Elephant, my little marble elephant, gift from Louis after his trip to
    India, mottled orange & black & grey, something like a calico cat,
    orange trunk curled down & touching his forefoot, sign of good
    luck, calico-colouring of good luck, lighting up days when they
    are colourless.

He wanders, the same way as my mother wanders, she who last
    year made a collage of family photos for my daughter's
    thirteenth birthday:
there's Chloe lying on the beach, buried up to her neck in sand,
    there's my dad holding Chloe's rag doll while she swooshes
    down a slide, there's Chloe & me arcing high into the air on
    swings, there's Chloe & her mom, ankle deep in the water as
    they stare out at an unmoving sailboat,
& there's one picture of my mother as a young girl (perhaps
    thirteen?), the only picture in black & white, it's a small picture
    at the top of the collage, my mother (standing in a snow-covered
    field, clump of trees in the background) lights up the landscape
    with her teenage smile,
at night, when we are all asleep, she steps from the snow-covered
    field, wanders midst the colour photographs, she unburies Chloe
    from her prison of sand, she takes the rag doll from my father &
    smoothes out her hair, she joins Chloe & me on the swings, three

  generations contemplate the unraveled calmness of Lake Huron,
my mother wanders midst our lives, her love has the strength of
  elephants, she holds up roofs, her smile illuminates the dark, her
  voice warms the cold,
she might not understand my desk & books, but she wanders midst
  the many words of our lives,
two months ago, her words came to an end, she now lies buried
  beneath the snow, a clump of trees in the distance, & I can't get
  over the feeling that one day I'll pick up the phone & hear her
  voice, my daughter will take one last swing to be pushed by her,
  my sons will teach her to kick a soccer ball.
I can't get over the feeling that, like my elephant, she is only hiding.

The Bones of My Mother

I am the bones of my mother
& the bones of my mother are in the ground
& in the branch stripped of leaves
& in the window that cannot be closed,
the bones of my mother fired with love,
the bones of my mother who threw out nothing, not even a paper
    bag, an elastic, a broken plate, after her mother died.

I am the bones of my mother
& the bones of my mother are in the winding roots
& in the stones lapped by the purling water
& in the door that I push through every day,
the bones of my mother buttressed by dreams,
the bones of my mother who braved her sometimes difficult children.

I am the bones of my mother
& the bones of my mother are in the whirling snowflakes
& in the coat that I throw on
& the pockets I stuff my hands into,
the bones of my mother brittle from her many fears,
the bones of my mother who, injected with Haldol, sank into a coma
    & never got a chance to say goodbye to her husband of 53 years.

I am the bones of my mother
& the bones of my mother are in the wind that blows from the north
& in the smoke that floats from the chimneys
& the knife that I hold in my hand,
the bones of my mother, I felt that singing was her natural state,
the bones of my mother who sometimes turned to stone when
    overwhelmed by disappointments.

I am the bones of my mother
& the bones of my mother are in the day that falls into night
& in the socks that I pull on every morning
& in the love that I have for my children,
the bones of my mother, the years hardened her gentle soul,
the bones of my mother who lost her smile but I'd phone her at all
    hours just to hear her laugh.

I am the bones of my mother
& the bones of my mother are in the birds that give the sky shape
& in the bricks that shelter another family
& in the slender grass that parts the sand,
the bones of my mother, storehouse of all her children's words,
the bones of my mother who saw her younger self in my daughter.

I am the bones of my mother
& the bones are caught in my throat,
I gasp for air, breathing will never be the same,
for I am the bones of my mother
& the bones of my mother rest in the earth;
a bird sings, its song swallowed up by the swollen clouds.

Hume Cronyn

III

Starbucks' Holiness

A middle-aged man wildly expatiates on the brilliance of the Compaq Computer ad which he single-handedly discovered the other night on TV while watching the Olympics. *All is holy.*

A square-jawed man reveals how his loquacious wife left him a three word note & a half-emptied house when she walked out on him April 1st. *All is holy.*

A teenager laments that she is evil, but her friend reassures her that she is only energetic. *All is holy.*

A thirty-something woman with a flamboyant silk scarf wrapped around her neck recounts the nail-biting drama of a Sunday purchase of a new Mercedes SL280. *All is holy.*

Painfully, a couple confides to an unlistening work colleague how their four-year-old daughter consistently misreads the word, *Doberman,* as *dog. All is holy.*

An ecstatic woman announces to her two university friends that today is a special day in the annals of history – Jell-O is a hundred years old. *All is holy.*

A teenage guy who has buried his three companions with his non-stop blather about music crowns his efforts with the announcement that John Zorn spends six months of every year in Japan subjecting his body to the flesh-tearing rigour of the whip. *All is holy.*

Bald head as shiny as a hockey helmet, a pink-socked man confesses his adoration for Canadian hockey because it is the closest thing we have to a religion. *All is holy.*

A woman in a flawless leather jacket & leopard-skin leotards recounts how she and her mother searched the length of Germany for this delicious perfume that has nine different fragrances. *All is holy.*

A teenager waxes eloquent about his paradise, Rejavik, Iceland – how it has 13 daily newspapers & one quarter of the population is under 20. *All is holy.*

Hume Cronyn

A long-haired guy confides to his equally long-haired friends that he wears boxer shorts because – and he momentously pauses – because he needs structure. *All is holy.*

A sandals-wearing teacher reverently declares to an accountant-looking colleague that the fundamental pitch of a Tuvan Undertone Singer is so low that it makes one's feet vibrate. *All is holy.*

Two women praise the roominess of their coats, but grow testy when they, examine the labels & discover that one coat withstands colder temperatures than the other. *All is holy.*

A woman enthuses about the irreplaceable value of her nanny – how there are days on end when the nanny won't allow her to hold her baby because she's too stressed out. *All is holy*

Fuck holiness! It's time to head down to the Lost Camel & knock down a few jugs of beer while listening to the buzzed misery of croaking flies.

Break My Life

Break my life on a dime.
Roll the dice and count three times.
Slide me a look, but don't wear my shoes.
Shake my hand, but forget my name.
Change the clothes of history, but throw me your rags.

Where's your good looks, mister?

Twenty-six. I look forty-five.
I roll over in my sheets.
I sink.
Hey look, there's a bird.
Its wings have been ripped off by two marauding men.
Call them God and the devil.
Its yellow beak once shone like the sun.
Now it lays at my side like a bayonet of lost dreams.

A dog barks. A man is bitten.
An earthquake kills a million people.
Cancer eats up bones as if they were rice crispies.
Does God enjoy fast deaths or slow deaths?

I have dug holes in the sand, found nothing but God's shit.
Millions are buried in His shit soon as they are born.
Why is one man's good luck, another man's bad luck?
The meek shall inherit the earth. That will never happen.

I can't stand it.

Break my life.

Hume Cronyn

When She Senses I Need Space We Sit at Different Tables

& the old lady in the middle of the room,
she's just bought change purses for her two grandsons who she's
 waiting for,
she's been saving pennies all week long so the change purses have
 something in them,
the pennies are stuffed in her coat pocket, which hangs over the back of
 the chair,
& just as she takes another sip of her Starbucks' coffee, two ladies brush
 against her chair,
her coat falls & pennies, cascading from her pocket, roll across the
 hardwood floor
&, as if they were drawn to the light, they roll towards the plate-glass
 window which gives one the view of a smashed-up column, hit by
 a car & now being noisily repaired.
The pennies roll &, as if on some invisible string, not one of them has
 fallen on its face,
they roll, oh, how they roll: they are her brunette hair turned white,
 they are the coldness of her freckled hands, the blindness of her
 one eye, loneliness that sits midst people sipping coffees from far
 off places, fingernails that break while trying to peel oranges,
& the pennies roll . . .

& me, sitting in the corner, devouring a Penguin anthology of American
 poetry, wanting to complete a story that I'm writing for the
 children, hankering after the wisdom of Eastern Religions,
 drinking an enormous coffee from a glass mug,
I watch the pennies of my mother-in-law roll across the floor,
I watch her get down on her knees, the two ladies flustering around
 her,
I can see my sons getting out of the car in the parking lot,
the man repairing the column, packing up his tools,
I am mesmerised as two pennies roll beneath an immaculate piano with
 a five-sticked candelabra balanced on its lid
(what is a grand piano doing in a joint like this?),
one penny falls & I roll with the last: that penny her kindness, her one
 eye that is not blind, the years her grandmother dressed her up as
 a boy & fled from one city to another, years that lose count, her
 independence & dependence all rolled in one,
& when the last penny falls, I jump up & go over to her,
she seems surprised at my appearance & ecstatic that she's found a
 quarter midst her pennies.

———————————   Don't Ask Me   ———————————

Santa Is Black & a Woman & Shoppers of the Dufferin Mall Have Seen the Light

Santa is black & a woman & she is walking through the Dufferin Mall,
the businessman with his white hair, he is so stern he will not allow himself to smile,
the bored salesgirl in the Jean Machine, the titillated customers who clasp packages of penis pastas or boob gummies in their hot, excited hands, the hustle & bustle of shoppers who are pouring Second Cup coffees down their gullets to sustain "shop till you drop" momentum, the man who clutches a two iron in the golf store & speaks to it like a lover, the woman who flops down in the leopard-skin inflatable couch with an exhausted sigh,
oh people! how many refuse to smile, staunchly refusing to let surprise enter their life, as if they smiled they'd break their jaws & come crumbling down in a big, or not so big, pile of bones,
ah, the women at the Body Shop, they may support green causes, they may decry the destruction of the rain forest, but damn it! they're not going to break their perfect lips & smile.

Santa is black & a woman & speaks french & shoppers of the Dufferin Mall have yet to see the light,
the teenager who mans the HMV counter, he looks like Johnny Rotten, don't want to tell him that Anarchy in the UK happened twenty-five years ago – today there's anarchy in the Dufferin Mall & he doesn't even . . . he doesn't even have a bone of anarchy in him, a tooth of anarchy, a fingernail of anarchy to wave, or smile, or grin, or even to move his lips one fraction of an inch to acknowledge that Santa is black & a woman, etc, etc,
what about the man staring at the diamond rings? even if he did smile you couldn't detect it beneath his huge, drooping moustache,
the two women standing outside of Joe's No Frills, God damn it, they don't even look up!
but Santa in all her grace, in all her ebullience, in all her polychromatic radiance, she smiles! she waves! she ho-ho-hos! she wishes everyone a Merry Christmas!

Santa is black & a woman & speaks french & amazingly shoppers of the Dufferin Mall begin to see the light,

Hume Cronyn

the ponderous, weighty molecules of consumerism, the drib & drab
    & depressed mentality of Christmas shoppers, the dense cloud
    that wraps us up & makes us only half human, the cloud lifts!
    – the blood-sucking, the limb-sucking, the spirit-sucking cloud
    lifts!
the woman selling African statues from her makeshift stall at the
    heart of the mall, she waves a pale, delicate hand,
the man selling Chinese vases, he smiles,
& standing in front of the vases, the big, bellied Buddha with his
    crazy gaping smile, hands lifted above his head, a golden ball
    held in each hand, I swear that He throws them up in the air, I
    see a spray of light that glints off the air-born balls,
& what about the toddler strapped in his stroller, who could ever
    forget his smile?
the seven Greek men sitting on the bench, one after another they
    smile, as if Santa had slipped chocolate-covered cherries in their
    mouths,
& the grey-haired woman in her wheelchair, she merrily chats to
    Santa in Italian, she kisses Santa's hand, Santa throws her arms
    around her & gives her a munificent hug,
oh, Santa is black & a woman & speaks a language that Dufferin Mall
    shoppers have rarely heard before, but oh how they open up,
    they open up like a shining funnel of sun & we all slide down it
    to some hallowed ground.

Blind Man

Blind man, who has led you to the middle of the street
& left you stranded on the white line?

Blind man, tapping with your cane,
is each step the one before you fall?

Blind man, take my arm,
how much trust do you put in the leading?

Blind man, when you walk into a room,
can you sense the height of ceilings, the glare of unsheathed light
    bulbs?

Blind man, when you sit at a table,
how urgent is your need to trace its shape, feel its texture?

Blind man, do you have perfect sight in your dreams,
have you ridden the wind across the black steppes of Russia?

Blind man, how sweet does the voice of a bird sound,
does the voice of evil corrode, how sounds the voice of kindness?

Blind man, when the sun shines on your face,
do you hear the angelic choirs of silence?

Blind man, does night lie on your shoulder like a broken wing,
does morning open you up like a crocus?

Blind man, can you tell the distance of walls,
& do most people seem like walls to you?

Blind man, the ticking of a clock at night,
a sneeze, laughter, do they erupt like a volcano in the whorls of your
    brain?

Blind man, touch my face, take your two hands & touch it,
what picture forms in your mind?

Blind man, it's whispered you put out your eyes with a pencil,
what pain brought you to that point?

Hume Cronyn

Blind man, when I see you I think of the wisdom of Tiresias,
I also think of the overwhelming loneliness of old people.

Blind man, hold tightly onto my arm,
take me somewhere I can't see.

The Mother of Jeff Buckley Laments

She went down to the river to sit on her toes & drink from a blade of grass purple as the wandering cows.

She longed for the cows to settle beneath the trees & low their gravitas songs, but she was pierced by the haranguing of irate fathers & the monotonous mastication of sandwiches being munched.

Her ears were picking up every sound: loneliness sliding down the leather of bucket seats, people praying to the immaculate conception of ice cubes.

She took off her clothes & her kneecaps. The wild mushrooms bellowed. Tree trunks pleaded for lovers to cut initials into their trembling bark.

She took off her lips & hung them around her neck. She stuffed stones into her mouth.

The wind grew prickly in her skin.

She saw her child at the bottom of the river. With that most beautiful voice of his, he was singing Glorias to the catfish suckled by the mud.

She forgot about the cows, the munching of sandwiches, people smitten by ice cubes. The river flooded its banks & took her home to her child.

IV

Stigma

Stigma that excludes instead of includes,
stigma that distances instead of approaches,
stigma that disfigures instead of making beautiful,
stigma that destroys instead of creates, that harms instead of
 harmonizes, that brands with tears of fire instead of letting loose
 the hawks of genius,
stigma that disables & dismantles, that digs deep & wide & even more
 till there is no place to stand but the basement of shame,
stigma that distrusts,
stigma that attacks,
stigma that blinds,
stigma that ruins/shatters/ravages,
stigma that forces you to wear a yellow star/stand at the back of a bus/
 tosses you from the burning window instead of celebrating our
 many differences,
stigma that starves instead of nourishes,
stigma that chains & chokes & confines instead of opening out,
stigma that punishes,
stigma that violates,
stigma that terrorizes,
stigma that abuses/confuses/refuses,
stigma that tosses out a few coins in its charitable mood instead of
 caring,
stigma that buries you six feet under & calls it living,
stigma that teaches you to drown & calls it swimming,
stigma that disembodies instead of embodying all the wondrous
 talents that live within us,
stigma that discombobulates, that twists & crumples & crimples the
 piano strings instead of nurturing the soul's many sonatas,
stigma that breaks you at the knees/the arms/the neck & a hundred
 other places & calls it healing,
stigma that pulls down the clouds & blankets a whole population in
 greys,
stigma that closes doors, windows, closes your mouth, dams up your
 idea stream, don't utter a contradiction – the safety of the
 community is at risk!
stigma that hates instead of loves,
subtracts instead of adds,
refracts instead of illuminates,
stigma that burns & torches & runs down the spine like scalding
 water,

Hume Cronyn

stigma that loses control & swallows up more & more people,
stigma that shrinks life, diminishes life, practices a scorched earth
    policy – what do they have against the holy fields of our
    plenitude?
stig that is STIG
& there's no MA in the word,
especially if you're stigmatized in this
    motherless/motherless/motherless world.

"Will You Take Me Home With You?"

There is so much rage in me. Last night I couldn't stop walking around the kitchen table. I felt like my body was steeped in gasoline and if I stopped pacing a match would drop and I'd fly open with an explosion of flames that would blister the sky.

A week ago, a man came into my office. The day before that, he had stood in the drop-in centre and punched his temple over and over, and each time his head had snapped sideways touching his shoulder. Then he had grabbed the corners of his mouth and pulled so hard that it began to bleed. When he came into the office, he was crying. Not huge dramatic sobs, but the weeping of innocent children who have been clearly wronged and have been crying for hours. Then his face went flat, absolutely devoid of emotion for several seconds, before he started to cry again, words tumbling out of his mouth, "I've been born into this world, but I have no mother, I have no father. I'm so small. God is so large. He'll look after me, won't he? WON'T HE?"

I am now sitting in the art room at the centre. I am surrounded by paintings on the wall: naked women bent over and angular in their hunched-up pain; women with enormous hands trying to tear out the shadow that dominates their heart; a fragile man lost on a terrifying shore of shale; a woman with bleeding lips. I'm thinking about the gift of love: love from our parents, lovers, friends, children. Without it, life is a total lie, a total deception. Love allows hope to enter into the minutes of the day. Everything is possible. We run with the light, build mountains, study the silence, and string words to the heavens. Love allows us to create life rather than being pawns frantically traversing a greasy chess board.

But who has ever had that love? I mean real love. That's what that man was crying out. He was falling to impossible depths. He was falling down the dark light of his vertabrae. He was falling into truth.

Hospitals, his long-lost parents, people on the street call this man mentally ill. But I have never heard anyone speak about loneliness so lucidly, so poetically. And what shall we call ourselves, we who are cowards, too afraid to admit to our loneliness, too afraid to admit to the deep-rending pain of our heart? Instead of uttering the scream from the bridge, what do we do? We bury our pain beneath our stultifying seriousness, the rigidity of our shoulder blades, the dead light of our eyes, the pavement of our touch, the claustrophobic weight of our songs, the gunny sacks of our bodies, the potato dust of our ideas.

This man in his falling. What terror had he seen? One day, he came in with bars of blood across his face. He had clawed his face with ragged fingernails. Later that day, when I was going home, he grabbed hold of my hand and cried out, "All I do is listen. You know what I mean. I might as well be a statue. Why was I given breath? Why was I given this mouth of mine? Why was I given these eyes? The blind are saved from seeing. A mute person is heard more than I am. I can't take it anymore. . . Will you take me home with you?"

And do you know what I said, "No, I have a wife and three kids. And we all sleep in the same room. But I'm always here for you." Pathetic! I'll walk the bridge forever. You'll find me muttering in the shadows. I know I can't take this man home. I know all the logical arguments. But nothing will change until this man is taken home and made part of our family.

Safety in the Streets

The wind was cold
as if an icy, grey water washed thru me.
I slept on a park bench, Allen Gardens,
another winter approaching.
A trapezoid of light watched over me,
it was mother/father, & the great God
above who looks after us.

WHACK.
A boot kicked into my back.
Knuckles crashed into my cheek.
I rose up swinging,
chopped one in the jaw, he didn't even teeter.
They flew at me, jab to the side of my head,
knee into gut, karate chop to neck.
NOSE BLEEDING.
Taste of blood.

Then one came back,
brick saw raised in his hand.
He slashed my lip, chipped one of my teeth.
I RAN. I ran where he couldn't catch me.
I pulled together my wound.
Then I turned around, waited till they found me,
then the real fighting began.

I'm 45.
I can't live this way any longer.
I need a rest, some place to stay for a few days.
I must gather myself up.
There are not too many years left to me.
I DON'T RECOGNIZE MYSELF ANY LONGER.

Do you think He'll recognize me?

Hume Cronyn

Ballad of a Lone Bag Man

Pigeons
were sitting on the eaves
of the A & P

He was a bag man,
bags hanging from neck
& shoulders,
one of them made from
a remnant of a fleece-
white carpet

Seeing the pigeons,
he thought how sad
they looked
He bought forty pounds
of sunflower seeds

sat on a low
wall, threw out
the seeds

in cascading arcs
they sailed through
the air and fell
to the ground

handful after handful

Pigeons descended
They only stopped
pecking when
they looked
up at him

He beamed
and chattered,
told them, You
can't buy
love, My
wife left me &

died on the sidewalk
from drugs, I
don't trust love,
Safety & respect
will do

They gobbled on
undisturbed He watched
the yellow ring around
their eyes, a
partial eclipse

He wondered if they
had intelligence,
whether they were
thankful? But he
doubted that

Why should
they be,
if humans had
never been in
his life?

Some weeks later,
he was walking
by the A & P

A guard dog,
a snarling wolf-
like dog,
bound across the parking
lot

charged
at him

was ready
to tear him
apart

Above his head,
a flock of pigeons

Hume Cronyn

appeared, hovered
like a squadron
about to
dive

The dog stopped
in his tracks
Went down on
his belly

Some kids saw the
whole thing Previously
they had pelted him
with stones

now, whenever
they see him, they
say hello
& sometimes
they slip him
a sandwich

Pop a Pill

If you're tired and you got a head ache, and the sun is shining in your
 eyes, and the trees look like great electrodes,
Pop a pill.

If you're trying to stop smoking and you're craving, and your fingers
 are popping, dying to hold a cigarette, and your lungs need the
 pure spirit of nicotine,
Pop a pill.

If you're lonely, and you only see yourself in the reflection of the
 window, and no footsteps are to be heard, and it seems you
 haven't been loved for years,
Pop a pill,
And if that does no good,
Pop another.

If your stomach is hurting and your back is aching, and you're about
 to turn thirty-four and you still don't know what you want to do,
 and every time you turn in bed you see the nothing of your life,
Well, pop a pill,
And quickly too.

If your nerves are bad and your roommate's drinking kerosene, and
 you're spending the night watching your hand jitter on the table,
 mesmerized by the knuckles bare of skin,
Well, it's not the only answer,
But it helps,
Pop a pill.

If you're cold and out on the street, and all the warm-air grates are
 occupied with the sad hunch of layered bodies, and the blue scarf
 is tightening around your neck,
Pop another pill,
Stelazine is your house,
Valium, your warmth.

If the salt of your life is burning like sodium on water, and every
 pore is an open window that suffers every glance, and every
 voice is whispering against you,
Pop a pill,
It will get better.

Hume Cronyn

If you've gained sixty pounds in a couple of months, and your tongue
 is sticking to the roof of your mouth, and the loops of flesh
 beneath your eyes are twitching,
Don't worry,
These are only minor side effects,
Quickly now, pop another . . .
God damn you, swallow it!

Miracle of a Warm Cob

Weeks later I returned to his room.
Nothing had changed.
His poems were scattered on the carpet
like clouds shot through with black pins.
I could never help it, but my eyes
were always drawn to the far corner
where the only colour in the room was a box of Tide.
Once, when I asked him why he bought the family size,
he laughed, said he had no family, only his demons,
and trying to keep their clothes clean was like trying to scrub the
 night.
The blankets on his bed were twisted from battle.

As usual he sat in his only chair,
a lone chair he called the pilot's seat.
He was staring above my head at a poster
that at first was quite difficult to make out:
it was the cockpit of an airplane,
unbelievably crowded with panels of intricate controls.
I sat on the floor looking at the puffed-up blue below his eyes:
somewhat a symbol of the always closed curtains, the stuffy air
and the perpetual night he lived through.

Finally, he spoke in that quiet, deliberate voice of his.
He said that he had been wandering for nights,
hungry, friendless, the leaves falling but never reaching the ground;
the streets glistening with iridescent splotches of gas burning into his
 eyes;
his hunger, big as night, gnawing at his stomach.
He had lost his coat. Shivering, he could imagine
every crease, the missing button, the frayed cuffs,
now a tiny hump on a bench he had slept on.
He didn't even know what city he was in.
A policeman on a horse gave him an apple
but he gave it to a little girl in a blue dress.
He saw an airplane fly through a tree.
He heard the leaves laugh.
Then he felt a hand and it led him home.

Hume Cronyn

The first thing he noticed when he entered his room
was his coat neatly folded on his bed.
He touched the coat to remember it,
then unfolded it: the smell was of summers ago.
Wrapped inside was a cob of corn:
a cob of glorious yellow, piping hot,
the steam warm on his face;
the steam nourishing his hunger.
He picked up the cob,
was going to take a bite, but couldn't.

For two months he carried the cob wherever he went.
It grew black: it reminded him of the mouths of old farmers.
It had a sweet, sickly, pungent smell
like the pages of an old bible.

And I looked at him.
I saw him shining yellow,
steaming with the piping of his story.
This man left too long in harsh, white pockets,
victim of clinical eyes and weekly injections, packed away in cell-like
        rooms,
his eyes were nourishing me, and the walls, and beyond.

How He Got There

Between the highway and the subway tracks, you can see a triangular patch of grass surrounded by an imposing wire-mesh fence. There appears to be no access to it, but true to all good mysteries, the grass is beautifully mown. From the window of the subway train a woman, a social worker, could see him on the grass. She thought it curious that he was directly under one of the two overarching lights.

It was almost midnight, she was on her way home, and he was on his hands and knees, searching for four-leaf clovers. When he found one, he plucked it and laid it in an old tin which once held tobacco.

An hour later, another passenger noticed him lying on his back. He was puffing a cigarette with the tin of four-leaf clovers on his stomach. The passenger thought he looked like a man on a well-deserved coffee break.

The man lying on the grass, married for three years, had just broken up with his wife. He was tired of sleeping 14 hours a day on medication; tired of living on the miserly amount of welfare that he received. His wife, alarmed by his turn of thoughts, told her psychiatrist who recommended that they separate.

Lying on the grass, he was thinking that he had collected 100 four-leaf clovers, he would sell them at 25 cents a piece, he smiled when he thought of his special – four for 75 cents. Tomorrow, he would sell them all. He tried to calculate how much he would make. Maybe $10? $15?

A man must have money before he gets a job. He was 51, hadn't worked for years, had made an application to a company that advertised to hire 2000 chronically unemployed. He knew they wouldn't look at him unless he had a new shirt, shoes!

When he got back to his place, he laid down on his bare mattress and pulled the one blanket he owned over himself. He could hear the mice running in the walls. His floor was covered with four-leaf clovers turned brown, TV sets, an electric fan, an industrial-sized coffee percolator, a child's wagon, and numerous garbage bags full of clothes and other things that he'd found while combing the streets.

Hume Cronyn

Every weekend he would drag the whole lot onto his landlord's lawn and stick up a flimsy sign in penciled letters – YARD SALE. So far he had only sold a crepe pan that he thought was a frying pan.

It was two in the morning, it would soon be Saturday, he had a new 26 inch TV which he had bought yesterday for $20, but which he was sure he could sell for $400 as soon as he fixed it. He pulled out his last cigarette. It had taken him an hour to bum it, but he couldn't go to sleep without a final cigarette.

He woke up in hospital. The walls of his basement room were black with smoke. In the child's wagon – untouched by the flames – the landlord angrily wheeled out the burnt man's possessions and dumped them in the gutter.

Parc Camping Trip(II)

I am a silent man.
Once I loved to talk
beneath the cracked lights
and the pale flow of beer.
I would talk and talk
till the morning streamed through the windows.
Now I listen,
and sometimes when I listen
I feel like a speck of sawdust
that is raised up and exalted like a westward-leaning jack pine.

This is the story of words,
words sung,
and sung,
they flew up like fireflies
and lit up the cold sky.

We sat around the campfire –
Margo, Michelle, Bob, Rick, Eric and ten others.
The fire flickered; faces glowed;
shadows were held back
like dogs on leashes about to leap.
And we were embraced,
embraced by the warm fire,
embraced more fully than any lover could ever hold us.
In the city we are called glueheads, schizophrenics, nutbars, manic
           depressives, loonies,
but out here,
out on the point lapped by water,
out beneath the stars and the pine trees redolent with resin,
we sit on rough-hewn logs,
sit shoulder to shoulder
and sing.

We sing for ourselves,
we sing for the person next to us,
we sing for lives that have been a parched throat.
Our voices, at first, reticent mumbles, awkward attempts,
voices oppressed by medication, hunger, homelessness,
voices that have not sung for years,

Hume Cronyn

suddenly they gain strength,
and gaining strength, we populate the sky with the words of our lives,
we populate the sky,
for once the sky is for us,
not for the skyscrapers, traders of flesh, merchants of venom, parasite
       lawyers, cop-out politicians,
but for us, the sky is for us!
Each word is our signature,
and it is carried by the wind:
some child will wake up in Iran and hear our voices,
some mother living in a Yangtze River cave will catch a fragment of our
       song,
some old man, once battered by Chilean truncheons, will fall asleep to our
       song.

The song finishes. Each one of us feels a quiver of fear. What will rush into
       the gap?
Nothing! Those fuckers who sit in hospitals and label us, those unmerciful
       children who dog our heels, those callous ones who ghettoize us,
they are held at bay, for once we are what we are,
not labels, but the undeniable gift of soul-life.

Bob thumbs through a battered old folk book, looking for another song.
I sit next to him. He mumbles, points to a song. I say yes.
He strikes a chord, the first words.
Michelle and Margo, next to me, pick up the words,
sing the most delicate harmonies, like wounded hummingbirds.
I follow up. Eric joins in, Rick, D.J., Brenda,
our voices gain the confidence of Gothic cathedrals,
'Corrina, Corrina, where'd you stay last night?'

The ancient forming of the rocks calls us a gathering of angels,
the wind through the trees calls us a window of light,
the lapping of the water calls us the venerable pilgrims of experience,
and the sky bends down to be part of our singing,
a star is found in each chest,
and the wind bows to the pain of our voices.

V

An Ordinary Evening

When I put on my hat,
all the birds fly in circles,
the sabre-tooth tiger wanders back to his lair
& the little girl who prayed for a unicorn on her sixth birthday
finds one grazing in the hallway.

When I walk down the street with my hat shining in the setting sun,
the street lamps swivel their hips,
the puddle I step in meows like an Assyrian cat,
a cloud sails by in the shape of an open mouth
& Tiresias, that ancient sage, stumbles out of a darkened alleyway
to proclaim that men and women love sex equally
and twenty-four hours in a day is not enough.

When I arrive at my girlfriend's,
I float across the water of the door,
she turns on a pot of Neptunian tea,
scent of fennel as our clothes fall like leaves,
the last candle burns out,
the window shines like a pearl
&, as the bell holds its note,
we swim out on a single thread of hair.

Song of Solidarity

Crazy necks of fire have stolen my licence plates.
It could've been worse. They could've stolen my wallet,
but what would they want with brick dust
& a park bench donated by the local funeral parlour?

What's a park bench doing in my wallet?
I couldn't stand it perched on the hill
overlooking the playground. Would you sit
on a bench donated by a funeral parlour?

Well, lots of people do.
I've seen them so bored with life
that even the play of children isn't enough.
So what do they do?

They stand up & touch their toes –
some crazy New Age belief
that a cranial blood bath cleanses
the spirit & refires the emptiness.

It's then that their necks jump with fire
& out of sheer craziness they rip off my licence plates.
They think I'm going somewhere.
In truth, I'm no different than them.

Hume Cronyn

Pears

Please don't disturb!
A man in here
Is eating some lettuce
And a fruit
With the most delicate ears.

Pears
Hear everything that is said.
They must be eaten in silence.

With a knife
Cut stairs
That wind around the pear.
Walk up the stairs
With a candle:
The flicker of light
Is lost in the white pulp.
Nothing is seen.
Nothing is heard.
All is taste.

Taste
That sweeps through the body,
Grows larger than the body,
Encloses
The body in one large pear.

Shhh!
That man is a pear.
Few people know such delight.

Walking on Water

The rock was a sheer black slab of rock, a midnight rock, a pitch-black rock with a gash of red that looked like an open wound. I stood on the rock. It was cold on my feet. I stood there, looking out over the lake. The rock sent a chill through my body. The water was blue & green but, where the wind lashed up the white caps, yellow puffs hung above the water like mysterious, ancient lanterns. I saw a path across the water with lanterns lighting the way. The rock told me to stay. It rooted my feet in their solidity. I looked up at the sun. It was an enormous red ball hanging in a yellow sky. The sun called to me. I had been standing still too long. *Take a chance*, it whispered. *One life is not enough, live many lives*. The wound in the rock festered. The sky flickered like a multitude of candles. The sun, bathing me in a pulsating light, hung like a huge heart of hope. I took one step, then another. The water held firm.

Hume Cronyn

Praise Poem

Take an orange.
With your thumb
rub its smooth but pitted surface.

Dig in your thumbnail,
peel away the rind.
Treasure the squirts of juice that splash your hands.
Note the web of whitish veins that wrap the inner orange.
Breathe in the sweet, bathing fragrance.

Take a section, hold it in your mouth.
Pop the skin with a tender toothbite –
mouth, flooded with the succulent flow of juices.
Forget your thirst for a moment:
wash it around your mouth,
then let it slide down your throat –
river of juice; fantastic, tumbling river of juice.
From what mountain does it flow?
How much sunshine lives in that river?
What blue skies?
Branches that suck in blue wind & turn it to orange roundness.

If you see me tomorrow & I am full of bubbly sunshine,
if I have a full head of hair & roses grow from my hands,
if my feet are turned inside out & I am eating a bank of nimbus clouds,
I am not high on crack or hash,
I am not drunk on 12-year-old scotch,
I am not riding the horse of my pierced skin,
I am not flying on the leaf of some exotic plant,

I had an orange for breakfast & finally tasted it.

Lake Muskoka

End of summer.
We are packing up, cleaning the cottage, storing the outdoor furniture
for the winter.
Last night: thunder storms
a continuous Muskokan growl
the children had clung to their mother.
I have just finished putting back the fallen screen window
cleaned the eaves troughs of pine needles.
My mother-in-law has taken the family out for lunch.
I remain behind, my last chance to sit on the rock.

The sky
white with puffs of light grey
like the inside of an oyster shell flecked with ashes.
The water
a grey calmness
a darker colour where the shoreline trees are reflected.
The quietness of water lapping
the odd bird
the rain from last night still dropping from leaf to leaf.
It's the last time this year
that I'll gaze across the lake
the cottages on the far shore as small as specks
the last time
before the city crowds in
slabs of buildings
asphyxiant air
jackhammers working throughout the night
evenings swallowed up by the children's homework
and the eerie quietness of now
another universe
I'm almost unable to link them.

I'm soaking up the quietness
a motorboat cuts across my peace, a white knife
another boat further out
and then back to this unnerving peacefulness
– what should be so natural is so unnatural –
this grey calm
this breathing water

Hume Cronyn

whose surface suggests the slightest rolling motion
whose surface cannot disguise the turbulent force which lives
underneath.
I'm storing its surface calm in me
storing its vital depths
storing the distance across the lake
storing the sound of the raindrops
storing all that which the noise of my day-to-day life paves over
storing all of this
and my body, giddy, is full of awe.

VI

Walk down the Milky Way

Today, we walked down the Milky Way,
no galactic walk, but a walk through a Parkdale alley,
at its mouth an abandoned sweater that looked like a rat,
I kicked at its tail, you popped a gum drop into your mouth & said
    that a good Buddhist would rescue that sweater, for there are too
    many people freezing on the street.
The wind caught a plastic bag, drove it into my legs.
Dust whirled. A crow, perched on the hydro wires, watched us with a
    cold eye.
Slammed into the back door of the hardware store, a shopping cart
    filled with two computer screens, pieces of lumber from a
    broken skid, a hub cap that threw up glints of light whenever the
    sun emerged from the clouds.
We stopped in front of a garage door, a rippled brown metal with
    FUCT painted in large gold letters, & stared at the Day-Glo gold
    till it shimmered into three dimensions.
You said, How often we look at things & only see them flat.
I expected you to go on, you usually spoke in a flood of words, but
    you had turned around
& were gazing at a dull, silver corrugated fence, with vertical strips of
    rust, which looked like tear drops that had slowly dripped from
    the top of the fence to the bottom.
I knew you were thinking of the tragic sculptures of Giacometti,
    pencil-thin because the horrors of war had stripped humankind
    of its spiritual weight.
We went on, jumped when a garage door was flung open, two
    smallish men darted out & started to unload a van. At first we
    could not decipher what the boxes were, then smiled with
    surprise – written on the side of the door, in large red letters,
    LIVE BAIT.
We were both fish of some sorts, we had spent a life of swimming,
    underwater was our medium, our oxygen was dreams, often
    times the reality of life was too much for us.
We veered off the alley, were surprised when we discovered an alcove
    that was perfectly swept, cedar fences backed onto it, each of the
    houses boasted a pine deck, a barbecue declared itself on each
    deck, a BMW was parked in one of the driveways.
We quickly retraced our steps, dove back into the dust & tattered
    plastic bags & rain-soaked pizza boxes & soggy brown leaves.

A ruffling sound interrupted us. Jerking our heads to the right, we
 saw three ghost-like figures hovering against a grey wall.
I had seen one of them before, the one in the blue duffel coat.
What I remembered about him was the inside lining of his coat was
 ripped & hung from the back like the tail of a whipped dog.
It was eerie, his hood was up, his face seemed so far back in his hood,
 all I could see was his nose that looked like an axe-blade.
The other two, one was a native man, the other a woman, her face,
 raw pink & chapped.
It didn't seem possible, but they moved closer to the wall, as if
 attempting to fade into it completely.
The duffel-coated man stuffed something gleaming into his pocket.
He looked at us, spat out, Are you following us?
We slunk past, as if we were ghosts ourselves.

The alley dipped & we were once more out on the street. We stood &
 marveled at the mural painted on the corner building, a mural
 with a patchwork of green hills & yellow fields that rose to a
 blue sky. Both fields & hills were covered with flowers – black-
 eyed Susans, daisies, poppies, clumps of ferns. Beautiful,
 red-bodied, purple-winged butterflies floated through the air. In
 the midst of this bucolic scene, two crudely-painted signs, NO
 PARKING HERE 24 HOURS.
You rushed over & lay down in one of the four parking spots in front
 of the mural.
You laughed & said, I bet if I lay here long enough, those traffic
 bastards would give me a ticket. After a pause, you continued,
 What car do I remind you of?
Oh, an old 57 Cadillac, I replied.
You said, No, I'm not that pretentious, I think I'm like an old
 Volkswagen Bug.
Whatever, I said, & I was drawn back into the mural. For a moment I
 was soaring like those butterflies above those two obscene signs,
 my wings were warmed by the summery sun of the mural, but I
 was quickly brought down to earth when you kicked me,
all too quickly I realized it was the middle of November, soon the
 city would be blanketed in snow, that we were on the cusp of
 winter & today's warmth so much more precious the last for
 perhaps five months,
I offered you my hands & you jumped up, we continued walking, I
 kicked a tin can & it rattled down the alley, a smashed wooden
 chair lay crumpled in a door stoop, someone had written on the
 metal door, FUCK DA POLICE.

Looking up, we quietly observed the dilapidated second story, the
    stucco punched away & the exposed red brick showing through
    like diseased gums. Jutting out from this, almost touching each
    other, two enormous satellite dishes.
Neither of us said anything, but we both knew that this was yet
    another sign of the press of gentrification.
You turned away, sighted something white & gleaming, nestled in a
    pile of garbage bags,
you picked it up & cradled it – it was a pair of china hands clasped in
    prayer –
suddenly, much to my surprise, you raised it above your head, said,
    Prayer is open hands, hands open to this world, forgiving hands!
    & hurled it to the ground.

We came to the back of the new Community Health Centre, I'd heard
    rumours of how spacious the garden was behind it.
Do you remember the time we helped to build the Japanese Garden:
    from the ruins of a once-renowned printing company, we laid
    sod, dug ponds, constructed Japanese bridges, planted
    languorous willow trees, & sculpted rockeries tumbling with
    a profusion of colourful flowers. (I have always loved the sense
    of creating something out of nothing.)
We walked up to the twelve-foot-high fence that surrounded the
    garden, the planks were wedged so close together that we
    couldn't even get a sliver's glimpse of the garden.
You were outraged: What does it take to cut some portholes in the
    fence so that people can look in? Are they afraid someone will
    see their garden paradise &, heaven forbid, want to enter?
As we were walking away, a mantle of foxglove draping the top of
    the fence caught our eye, we turned around to face it squarely, a
    bushy mantle of snow, it seemed so lightly perched, like some
    Zen brush-stroke of illumination, weightless revelation that
    shone from the core.
Suddenly, we were pulled from our reverie, there was a scuttling, like
    a chase of dry leaves driven down the alley.
It was a woman, who I often saw on the streets,
always dressed in black, she wore one leather coat over the other, a
    supply of toilet paper flowered from her pockets, a black bell-
    shaped hat was pulled down over her eyes.
Once, last winter, I'd seen her picking up smashed icicles from the
    sidewalk & dropping them into the gutter.
Today, she was circling a spray of shattered glass,
I heard her muttering, Oh, the children will hurt their knees if they

fall, The birds could hurt themselves, They come down to eat
bread, then they fly up to the trees, They do nothing to harm us,
Why should we harm them?
We were at the end of the lane, before it emptied into the street,
the house, one in from the corner, its back wall was painted with a
mural, but it was so different than the other one:
it looked like the cross-section of a brain, vivid convolutions of blue
& green & brown & grey,
spray-painted on by graffiti artists whose smoke-coloured signature
was lazily scrawled in the lower right-hand corner: *aerosol
phantoms*.
You ran your finger along the green. Such a bold green, you said, it
reminded you of the birth of new ideas.
I was only half-listening as I watched the black-leathered lady, her
face, so white, her lips, a garish red, with infinite grace she was
picking up the broken glass & delicately placing it in her other
hand.

Again, we spilled out into the street, quickly scurried across it,
entered the alley, once again assuming that furtive stance, that
stalking stance, as if not part of the general membership of
humanity, but more on the margins, transgressors, in our case,
silent observers.
We stopped before the back of a building, a fence blocked our view of
the lower parts of it.
We both knew its history. Once, it had been a home to forty-seven
people, now, charred pieces of plywood boarded the windows,
the railing of the ramshackle-old balcony completely dismantled.
Once, there was a flowering tree that dropped leaves onto the
balcony,
now, the tree, a bare tangle of branches, from one of them hung a
blackened shirt that looked like an impaled pigeon.
Four years ago, a fire gutted the building, someone had poured
kerosene over a couch in the hallway,
thrown a match, two women had died in the upstairs' apartments,
the angry blaze of fire had swallowed them up, two precious gifts,
a man, jumping from the third story, had bounced off the roof of the
bus shelter & done irreparable damage to his brain,
the superintendent, who rented the room to the arsonist, plagued by
guilt & fear, has lived four tortured years on the street,
now, the residents are scattered throughout the city, they shiver in
their rooms, no one can be trusted.
You said, Four years that building has stood empty. The landlord

refuses to sell it for less than three million.

He's scum that guy, I blurted out, there's thousands homeless & that building stands empty. Just imagine if …

It was no paradise, you interjected. Do you remember Ken, suffering from diabetes, stuffed in a closet-sized, basement room, his window kicked out, prowling cats stole his food, but still it functioned as a community where people shared moments of pain & happiness.

Ya, I said, they helped each other, I heard lots about their communal breakfasts.

What sort of society do we live in, you shouted, where a landlord makes money off an empty building?

And then, being the odd fish that we are, you got dreamy, & I got dreamy. We excitedly talked about how wonderful it'd be to own this building. Like that garden we once worked on, we'd create from dereliction a house, not a rabbit warren of closet-sized rooms, but spacious rooms. We mentioned how the drop-in centre next door had built ten units of affordable housing on the third floor, how lives had been totally changed by having a space that offered hope for a better life, a space which declared at every turn that you're a worthy human being. Oh, we had such flights of fancy. The future residents would help design & do the renovations, there would be a communal kitchen when companionship was desired, there would be a music room, an exercise room, a computer room.

So we dreamed & embroidered, we walked & walked, devising plans of how we would gain ownership of the building, so fantastic our plans became, until both of us burst into laughter. I kicked at a stone & shouted with pain as it catapulted down the street.

We then separated. Both of us had to be alone with our thoughts which ate us up, we couldn't sleep for days, we were the brains on that wall, green for new thoughts, brown for apathy, grey for despair, blue for extravagant wild hope.